THEN & NOW®

ROGERSVILLE

OPPOSITE: Pictured is Main Street in Rogersville in the 1920s. (Historical Collection of George E. Webb Jr.)

THEN & NOW®

ROGERSVILLE

Randy Ball and Rodney Ferrell

We dedicate this book to the people of Rogersville, our hometown,
who share the love of our history and heritage.
Thanks to those who have helped preserve our past,
and thanks to the future generations who will carry on the tradition.

ISBN 978-0-7385-6758-7

Library of Congress Control Number: 2008943874

Published by Arcadia Publishing
Charleston, South Carolina

Printed in the United States of America

Then and Now is a registered trademark and is used under license from
Salamander Books Limited

For all general information contact Arcadia Publishing at:
Telephone 843-853-2070
Fax 843-853-0044
E-mail sales@arcadiapublishing.com
For customer service and orders:
Toll-Free 1-888-313-2665

Visit us on the Internet at www.arcadiapublishing.com

On the Front Cover: A crowded Main Street in Rogersville in the 1940s included the Roxy Theater, commonly called just "Roxy," and the Hale Springs Inn. The inn had a modern sign out front, and *Key Largo* was playing at the Roxy. By 2004, the Roxy was gone, but the inn is still a Main Street icon. (Now photograph by Randy Ball; Then photograph from the Historical Collection of George E. Webb Jr.)

On the Back Cover: The Rogersville Post Office has not changed much since this 1950s image was made. (Historical Collection of George E. Webb Jr.)

Contents

Acknowledgments

It is an honor, a privilege, and a blessing to be able to complete Then & Now: *Rogersville*. This book is truly a dream of ours and a summary of much of our work about Rogersville. Years of research and photography have brought us this far, but we also owe a huge debt of gratitude to many people.

Thanks to George E. Webb Jr. for allowing us access to his collection of early Rogersville images. Most of the older images are in this book due to George's boundless generosity. George gave the use of his collection as well as sharing his historical knowledge in the many hours he helped with this book. Thanks to Cary Lewis Barton, Denver Price, and others who shared photographs and the stories behind them.

Special recognition must go to Henry Price, former Rogersville historian, who has been a huge influence on both of us. We hope collectors will find this work worthy and add this book to the vast body of Rogersville reference works that Henry has so ably produced. Many of the historical photographs were taken by the late Johnny Rowan, who was known as "Rogersville's photographer" for decades (as was his father before him). Thanks to the Rowans, so many great photographs of Rogersville have survived for us to enjoy.

Maggie Bullwinkel of Arcadia Publishing deserves special recognition for believing in the project and in us as writer and photographer. Her kindness and patience have made the completion of this book a reality.

Finally, thanks to our families and close friends for their support, patience, and love.

Photography Credits

The Then photographs are from the Historical Collection of George E. Webb Jr., unless otherwise noted. All Now photographs are by Randy Ball.

INTRODUCTION

Rogersville, Tennessee, is a quiet little town in the Appalachian foothills. The state's second-oldest town, Rogersville was founded in 1786. In its early history, the land that is now Rogersville was part of North Carolina, the lost State of Franklin, and finally Tennessee. Rogersville is named for early settler Joseph Rogers, and among its early citizens was David Crockett, grandfather of Davy Crockett. Crockett and his family were killed by Native Americans near Crockett Creek.

Three early presidents visited Rogersville: Andrew Jackson, James K. Polk, and Andrew Johnson. Confederate general Alexander Peter Stewart was born here. Rogersville has a long and storied history, but this volume concerns the town since the introduction of photography.

The oldest dated photograph in this book is from 1857. This is relatively early for a photograph from a small town. We were so fortunate to find the treasures of the historical photographs we were able to choose from. Thankfully Rogersville had the Rowan family to document the town through most of the 20th century, as well as many individuals who photographed their daily lives through the years.

Rogersville has been the home of two colleges, though there isn't one today. The Civil War split many neighbors and families, and businesses have come and gone. Through everything, the one unchanging thing about Rogersville is the spirit of its citizens. Many of the young people in every generation leave Rogersville only to move back home.

Rogersville has seen a great many changes in its time. It has gone from a tiny frontier town to a farming community to an industrial town. Rogersville Synodical College, Swift Memorial Junior College, and McMinn Academy are all gone. The local high school has been in three different locations. In recent memory, the Roxy Theater, the Jolly Roger Drive-In, the Po' Boy Restaurant, the Southern Railroad trestle, the Dixie Queen Drive-In, and the Rogersville Milling Company have disappeared. While it would be impossible to document every change, this book will provide some insight to Rogersville's growth and the changes experienced.

A walk through Rogersville today is a wonderful experience. You'll find yourself thinking "if this place could talk . . ." It's been said a picture is worth a thousand words, so enjoy the trip through these pages, and see what the photographs of Rogersville have to say.

—Randy Ball, January 2009

CHAPTER 1

TOWN SQUARE

Like many small Southern towns, the town square is the center of activity in Rogersville. The Hawkins County Courthouse; Overton Lodge No. 5, Free and Accepted Masons; Colboch-Price Funeral Home; and the lawn of the former Miller Hospital occupy the corners of Rogersville's town square. Rogersville's town square is at the intersection of Main and Depot Streets.

The Hale Springs Inn is near the southwest corner of the town square. It was built in 1824 by John A. McKinney. It is currently undergoing renovations. A popular inn on the early frontier, it played host to many famous people in the 1800s, including presidents Andrew Jackson, James K. Polk, and Andrew Johnson. Its name comes from a mineral spring near Pressmen's Home. The inn was a popular stopover for travelers going to the springs.

Built in 1836, the Hawkins County Courthouse is the oldest original courthouse in the state. It sits on the southeast corner of the town square. It was designed in the Jeffersonian Colonial–style of architecture by John Dameron of Sullivan County and has seen many changes during the last 170 years. The fancy cornice work, the columns, and the three Palladian windows have caused the Hawkins County Courthouse to be featured in architectural publications.

Overton Lodge No. 5 is across Main Street from the courthouse. It was built in 1839 as a branch of the Bank of the State of Tennessee. The lodge was chartered in 1805 and named for John Overton, Andrew Jackson's law partner. In 1880, the lodge acquired this building. Unlike many Southern lodges, Overton Lodge No. 5 continued meeting during the Civil War. This allows Overton Lodge No. 5 to claim the distinction of being the oldest continuously operating lodge in Tennessee.

The original Kyle house was built in 1850 and was one of the most beautiful residences in Rogersville. Located on the corner of Main and Depot Streets, it included a law office and a log livery stable. In 1939, the house was sold to Hickman Kite Sr., who turned the home into an apartment complex. After many years of decay, Kite sold the property to Randall Price and Ray Colboch. Shortly afterwards, the old structures were razed. Today the business is known as the Colboch-Price Funeral Home.

Located on the corner of Main and Depot Streets is the old Farmers Hotel. The Kyle family built this unique antebellum structure in 1847. They used the same architects who designed the Overton Masonic lodge. Dr. Jacob Miller later used it as a hospital until his death in 1929. Tom Rogan operated his law office there, and it was also the home of E. A. Cope's School and Office Supply. Today it is owned by John K. Wilson and is used as a law office and apartment complex.

The Kyle house is located at 1[illegible]1 West Main Street. The 22-room home was built in 1837 for William Simpson. It was later acquired by the Kyle family, who had occupied a large home where the Colboch-Price Funeral Home now stands. It has at times been a rooming house. Today it is home to several businesses. The Kyle house accommodated Southern officers during the Civil War. The house is constructed of "Kentucky Blue" brick laid in the English style.

Main Street has seen some changes since the 1930s. The most obvious is the Citizens Union Bank building on the left. It has been renovated and is now a U.S. Bank. The courthouse lawn, always well maintained, is seen on the right. The painted Parks-Belk sign on the side of that building stayed much the same until the store closed. The large sign pointing the way to the Rogersville Motor Company was on the corner of the courthouse lawn.

The Hawkins County Courthouse has seen many changes since its construction in 1836. Perhaps the most dramatic change was the replacement of the original bell-shaped cupola with a New England–style cupola in 1929. The county government gradually outgrew the historic building, so an annex was added when the courthouse was joined to the former Parks-Belk building. This added much needed office space while maintaining the courthouse's historical integrity. It is the oldest operating courthouse in Tennessee.

The Hale Springs Inn was originally McKinney's Tavern. During the Civil War, the owners were staunch unionists, and it is said that the inn housed Union army troops. The inn was beautifully restored by the late Carl Netherland-Brown in the 1980s. It closed in 1999. At the time of its closing, it was the oldest continuously open inn in the state. Renovations are currently being done, including the replacement of the back section of the building.

The Masonic Temple was originally designed by Thomas Jones as a bank building. It has been recognized as an excellent example of Greek Revival architecture. It was completed in 1845 at a cost of $9,000. It has served as a bank, a funeral home, and an office building, and was home to the *Rogersville Review* newspaper from 1885 to 1892. It was extensively renovated in 1955, but the original cornices and decorations were carefully preserved and replaced.

The Roxy Theater was a part of growing up for Rogersville citizens. Located on Main Street next to the Hale Springs Inn, the theater was built in 1946, replacing the Rogersville Theater, which burned that same year. Kermit Stengle was the owner of both theaters. W. P. Miller was the manager, and his daughter Sarah Grace Miller later managed the Roxy Theater. In 1988, Carl Netherland-Brown purchased the Roxy Theater and razed it to build a small park for the Hale Springs Inn.

CHAPTER 2

DOWNTOWN

This photograph of Perry Smith (left) and Luther Hurd was taken in 1967 in front of the Masonic Lodge in downtown Rogersville. The whittlers' and loafers' benches on the town square have always been popular. Through the years, old-timers have made and discussed history as they lulled away the afternoons as time marched on.

In the 1940s, parking was allowed on both sides of Main Street. On Saturdays, parking spaces were at a premium. These images are from the intersection of Main and Depot Streets, looking east. The building on the right is now the courthouse annex. Among the businesses now gone are the City Drug Store, Simpson's Grocery Store, the East Tennessee Grocery Company, and Hales' Restaurant. As in many communities, downtown Rogersville is now often quieter than it was in the mid-1900s.

The present First Baptist Church on Washington Street was built in 1921 and has seen several changes in the structure. The Baptist church first came to Rogersville in 1853 and was located near this church, around the corner on Depot Street. That building burned during the Civil War. In 1890, the Rogersville Baptist Church was reorganized with 23 members. From these challenging beginnings, the church would grow to become a mother church, helping to start many churches throughout Hawkins County.

In the early 1900s, Hawkins County was designated to participate in an experimental Rural Free Delivery (RFD) mail system, one of the first in the nation. Over a period of time, this system opened up several post offices in the county, and, by the 1930s, nearly every community in the county had a post office. The U.S. Post Office on West Main Street in Rogersville was built in 1932. Once-a-day mail delivery to the residents of Hawkins County began in 1930.

By the early 1950s, parking was allowed only on the north side of Main Street. These images are from the middle of a block in the business district. Canvas awnings were popular in the historical photograph, while many buildings had been renovated in the modern image. The Astor Café, Sterling Jewelry, the Corner Drug Store, the White Store, and Lackey's Restaurant can be seen in the early photograph. By 2008, canvas awnings had made a comeback.

The Terry Motor Company was located on West Main Street in Rogersville. Founder and owner Joe K. Terry Sr. started his career in the automotive business in 1926 working for the Testerman Motor Company. In 1953, he went into business for himself and opened Terry Chrysler Plymouth Dodge. In 1990, the Terry Motor Company joined with Alex Looney Chevrolet and moved to a larger complex on Highway 11 West. Napa Auto Parts now occupies the old Terry building.

In 1934, the Citizens Bank merged with the Hawkins County Bank to become the Citizens Union Bank. In 1954, the bank built a new structure and used a warehouse on the back property while construction was being done. The building underwent major renovations in 1978–1979. Dominion Bank acquired the Citizens Union Bank, which was acquired by the First Union Bank, which merged into First Star, which was then acquired by the present U.S. Bank.

Rogersville City School sits on Broadway. When the building was constructed in 1849 it was the Odd Fellows Female Collegiate Institute. In 1892, it became the Rogersville Synodical College, a private Presbyterian finishing school for young women. The county school system then bought the campus. The original buildings were destroyed by fire in 1928; a new building was constructed, and it served as Rogersville High School until 1950 when the "new" high school opened. It then became Rogersville City School.

Early in the 20th century, cars and horses shared Main Street in Rogersville. The passage of time is observed by the presence of utility poles as well as the unpaved street in the historical photograph, where several stylishly dressed citizens can be seen on the sidewalks. All utility lines are now underground, and period "heritage" streetlights line the street. The Palace Theater and Fains Café are prominent in the early photograph. The large clock sign is at Clifton's Jewelers.

Located on the corner of Hasson and Main Streets, this Dutch-style brick house (pictured below) was built by Dr. William Walker during the 1830s. The Hale family of Rogersville purchased the house in the 1880s, and Robert Franklin "Kildy" Hale inherited the house in 1921. "Kildy," as Hale was affectionately known, loved to sit on his front stoop and talk to passersby. Fire ravaged the structure in 1971, and Kildy died as a result. His heirs sold the property to the First Baptist Church, which razed the house and made a parking lot.

Located in the historic district of downtown Main Street, the old A. B. Rogan home was built around 1870. For many years it was one of the most opulent homes in Hawkins County and was the scene of many elegant parties. An invitation to the Rogan home was coveted indeed. In the 1950s, Jack Taylor operated the Taylor Funeral Home in the old mansion. After many years of serving the community, the funeral business folded, and the structure returned to being a private residence.

The Clay-Kenner house is located at 403 East Main Street. It was built in 1835 by John A. McKinny as a wedding gift for his son Charles, who was killed fighting Native Americans before he ever saw the house. It is famous for its hidden room, which was used by the Clay family to hide valuables and themselves from the Union army during the Civil War. The home has been beautifully restored and now houses offices as part of the H. B. Stamps Library complex.

The Holston Electric building on Main Street was built in the 1950s and was used until a new facility was built just west of downtown. The building was then utilized as the Tennessee Technology Center, an industrial trade school, for many years. Today the *Rogersville Review* newspaper occupies the structure. The first newspaper printed in the state of Tennessee was the *Knoxville Gazette*, which was established and printed in Rogersville by George Roulstone on November 5, 1791.

The Dr. Jacob Eastman Miller mansion was built in 1902. Located on West Main Street, it was the home of the Miller family until Dr. Miller's death in 1929. It then fell into the hands of prominent judge Hal E. Portrum. The 18-room structure remained in the Portrum family until the property was sold to the First National Bank of Rogersville in 1957. An unfortunate victim of progress, the brick house was torn down to make way for the present bank building.

The Romoco Farm Store was an essential agriculture supply business, selling tractors and equipment on Depot Street for decades in the 20th century. In the historical image, the store is being used in a scene from *The River*, a major motion picture filmed in Hawkins County in 1982. It featured Mel Gibson and Sissy Spacek in the lead roles and included several local people. Later the Romoco Farm Store moved just outside of town. Now the building houses several small businesses. (Then photograph from the Randy Ball collection.)

Growers Warehouse was on East Main Street. It was one of three tobacco warehouses in Rogersville. Tobacco was Hawkins County's leading cash crop for most of the 20th century, and warehouses were where the farmers sold their crops to the tobacco companies each winter. With the decline of the tobacco-growing industry in the United States, two of the warehouses have been torn down, and the other is used for storage. The lot where this one stood remains empty. (Then photograph from the Randy Ball collection.)

Rogersville once had two flour mills located near each other: Rogersville Milling Company (Livesay's) and J. A. McDonald and Sons. They were located off Broadway across from Rogersville City School; both are now out of business. The grainery is now gone. The three-story frame building was said to be Rogersville's tallest structure. The brick building was used by the Rogersville Milling Company and was formerly a box factory. It now houses several offices and businesses. (Then photograph from the Randy Ball collection.)

The Pettibone House, which was originally Joseph Rogers Old Tavern House, stands at 207 South Rogers Street. It was a popular lodging place in Rogersville's early days. The house is actually made up of two log houses joined together and covered with siding, making it a "double house." It is next to the Joseph Rogers Big Tavern House. Both structures were built by the town's founder and are now owned by the Rogersville Heritage Association, along with the adjacent Crockett Springs Park.

The old Hawkins County Jail building was constructed around the beginning of the 20th century. Oddly enough, it is the third jail to occupy the corner of Depot and Washington Streets. The first jail structure was built of logs around 1800. Unlike the former jails, this building was rather unique because all the cells had windows. The structure was torn down and replaced with a parking lot. The new jail building was constructed on the corner of Washington and Church Streets.

The Methodist church was established in Rogersville in 1822. The first church was on Church Street, and the old cemetery is still located on that property and is the final resting place for many early citizens. A brick building (formerly the Hawkins County Farm Bureau) now occupies the site in the historical photograph. The present Rogersville First United Methodist Church on Colonial Road just off of Main Street was opened for worship in 1950 with Lon Moneyhun as pastor.

The International Playing Card and Label was founded in 1926 by George L. Berry. For more than 80 years, it was one of the premier employers in Hawkins County. Berry, who was the president of the International Printing Pressmen and Assistants' Union of North America, wanted a shop that could compete with printing shops in the North. In 2006, the company merged into Mundet International and finally moved all operations to a new plant site at Phipps Bend. Today the old International Playing Card and Label building stands empty and silent.

The Rogersville Presbyterian Church was formed in 1805. The first church was built in 1820. The church split into two congregations, the "old school" and "new school," in 1838 and reunited in 1881. The present church was built in 1840 at 309 West Kyle Street, and John Dameron was the architect for both buildings. The church bell was brought from Philadelphia. The church is known for its ornate interior and pipe organ, and the building was remodeled in 1927.

The Dobyns-Taylor Hardware building on Main Street has housed many businesses. Dobyns-Taylor Hardware, seen in this 1964 yearbook photograph, was one of several hardware merchants downtown in the 1950s and 1960s. It moved to this building from a location just down the street. For a long period in the 1970s and 1980s, the building was home to Ball Brothers, a furniture store. Today it is home to a variety of stores in an area named the Shoppes of Marketplace.

Main Street still follows the same contours as it did in this 1920s image. This view is from the east end of the downtown section, looking west. Among the long-forgotten businesses seen here are the Palace Theater and Fain's Café. The Brownlow building is in the foreground on the right. The large trees of the town square are seen in the background of both photographs. Also noticeable is the lack of traffic lights in the historical image.

Time has passed on Main Street. The Citizens Union Bank displayed a clock on the front of the building for years. The clock in this 1964 Rogersville High School yearbook photograph (below) was replaced in late 1969 by a digital clock that displayed the time and temperature. The U.S. Bank is now at this location, and no clock is on the building. The clock in the image at left is near the Citizens Bank down the street.

The Rogersville Depot is on the corner of Broadway and Depot Street. It was built in 1890 by the Southern Railroad company. The tracks in Rogersville came to a dead end just past the depot at the mill, where there was a turntable. Railroad commerce faded in the 1960s and 1970s. The tracks were removed in Rogersville, but thankfully the depot has been restored and now houses the Rogersville Heritage Association office and the Tennessee Newspaper and Printing Museum.

Founded in 1875, St. Marks was the first black Presbyterian church in Rogersville. Formerly located on McKinney Avenue, the church moved to the corner of Kyle and Hasson Streets in 1912. Rev. William H. Franklin, founder and pastor, served St. Marks and Swift Memorial College for many years and was buried on the Swift Memorial College campus in 1898. The church dissolved on July 21, 2002 Ella Jo Bradley, a Swift Memorial College alumni and former schoolteacher and civic leader, led the fight to save and preserve the structure.

The Armstrong house (now the Rogers-Burdette house) was the first house built on Broadway. It was constructed in 1875 and has been in the same family since 1899, when Florence Armstrong purchased the property. Current owner Janelle Burdette grew up here and returned in 2007. It sits on a beautiful, large, gently rolling lot. The house has remained in the family and has been renovated but still maintains its original historic charm. It sits at the edge of the Historic District.

There have been many changes to Main Street—even as recent as the 1960s. In this view looking west, some businesses now gone are the While Store, Dobyns-Taylor Hardware, Sterchi's Furnishings, the *City News*, Free-Service Tires, and the Corner Drug Store. Also of note is the highway junction sign on the right. Sidewalk construction was in progress in the photograph below, which was taken by the late Johnny Rowen.

Depot Street has changed completely since this *c.* 1929 image was taken. The residence with the fenced animal pen is gone. The Shanks Hotel, now gone, is the second building on the right. The Hale Springs Inn and the Hawkins County Courthouse are in the background of the historical image. In the time between the taking of the early image and the 2008 photograph, two longtime businesses on Depot Street had come and gone: local Chevrolet dealer the Rogersville Motor Company and the Romoco Farm Store.

Located on the corner of Colonial Road and East Main Street is Rosemont, one of Rogersville's most beautiful antebellum mansions. It was built around 1841 by John A. McKinney as a wedding present for his daughter Susan and her husband, John Netherland. The house has remained in the Netherland family since that time. Mr. and Mrs. Carl Netherland Brown purchased Rosemont in the 1970s and have since restored the old home to its original grandeur.

The First Christian Church of Rogersville was organized in the 1930s but had no regular house of worship until 1937. The North Methodist Church property, a small wooden building, was purchased for $1,250, and the congregation met in that building until 1948 when ground was broken for the present redbrick building. The congregation shown here is from the late 1950s. The church later acquired the adjacent property where the Shanks Hotel once stood.

The Citizens Bank of Rogersville operated for a time in the Masonic Temple. The bank then purchased the Lou Simpson property (originally the James Neill building) adjoining the town square and moved all operations there. In 1898, a new building was erected that also housed a post office. Though the names have changed over the years, a bank has been located on this spot, town lot No. 26, ever since.

The "new" Rogersville High School opened in the fall of 1950 with Don T. Pargo as principal. The high school classes were relocated from the building on the Rogersville Synodical College campus. It served as a high school until Cherokee Comprehensive High School opened in 1978. It then became Rogersville Middle School. This building has seen many homecomings, ball games, the first integrated classes, and community events, and it has survived a fire.

In the 1950s, Main Street in Rogersville was a busy place. Shown in this image looking east from the town square are Parks-Belk, the City Drug Store, Bendix Home Laundry, Dobyns-Taylor Hardware, Rod Armstrong and Company, Bowers Restaurant, the White Store, and Western Auto, which were all part of Main Street commerce. Today many of the same buildings still stand, but all these businesses are memories. Now most of the stores are on the edges of town, and offices and small shops occupy most of the downtown area.

The railroad was slow in coming to Rogersville. As early as the 1830s, east Tennesseans were excited about railroads, but Rogersville was not included in the railroads' initial plans. Early tracks went through Bulls Gap, but rail commerce finally came to Rogersville in 1867. The historical photograph shows the first coal-fired engine to serve Rogersville. Stationmaster Robert Webb is standing on the right. Sadly, the railroad is now gone, but the depot is now a newspaper and printing museum.

CHAPTER 3

Outskirts

The nearby countryside is as much a part of Rogersville as the downtown area. Many of the citizens and much of the commerce and heritage have existed just outside the city limits. Historic homes, mills, bridges, and country stores have been an important part of Rogersville's countryside.

The McDonald's Mill building was constructed in 1810 on the Holston River. It was originally McKinney's Mill, then Austin's Mill, then Spears' Mill, and finally McDonald's Mill. It was razed in 1966–1967. (Randy Ball collection.)

Located on Burem Road on the outskirts of Rogersville is the Amis house, one of Hawkins County's most historic homes. It was built by Thomas Amis in 1781 on Big Creek, near the stream's confluence with the Holston River. The stone structure was originally a compound consisting of an inn, a family dwelling, a school, a distillery, a post office, and a fort, all surrounded by a log palisade. Today the house remains in the Amis family and is in the process of being restored to its former grandeur.

The Andrew Jackson Inn was located on Highway 11 West, formerly the Old Stage Road, west of Rogersville. Robert Nall first built a large log cabin on the site. W. C. Kyle bought the property in 1850 and built a large brick mansion, the Green Tree, later known as the Evergreen. It was learned that the house shared the same craftsmen that worked on the Hermitage, and it later became the Andrew Jackson Inn. Razed after a fire in the 1990s, it is now the site of Quality Inn Suites.

The Stagecoach Inn was built in 1840 by James McClure. It was constructed near what is now Highway 11 West. The brick structure had 15 rooms and six chimneys. The inn was razed in the early 1970s when Burlington Industries bought the land to construct a manufacturing facility. The Burlington plant never opened, and the building was sold to TRW, a Cleveland, Ohio-based, automotive supplier, which has been one of the county's largest employers.

The Thomas Gibbons house is located 3 miles east of Rogersville. Gibbons was born in Surry County, Virginia, in 1734. He built this house in 1778. The court of the now-extinct Spencer County, State of Franklin, met in the house from 1785 until 1787. On June 4, 1787, the first county court of Hawkins County, North Carolina, met here. A Tennessee court was also held here. The house has been well maintained and is now used by a religious organization. Having been home to the courts of three states, it is one of Hawkins County's most historic buildings.

The log American Legion Hut was the second clubhouse built in Tennessee after World War I. According to the cornerstone, it was constructed around 1925. It officially became known as the "The Hut," and for many years it was the center of social activity in Hawkins County. It was torn down in 1950 to make way for the larger, more modern brick structure. For more than 50 years, the American Legion Memorial building served the community in many ways, including as a bowling alley and more recently as the Rogersville Playhouse.

The county bridge across the Holston River south of Rogersville connected McKinney Chapel Road with Highway 70. Just above this bridge, TVA built another bridge to handle construction traffic for the building of the John Sevier Steam Plant. The completion of the Hugh B. Day Memorial Bridge on Highway 66, a short distance below the County Bridge, caused a loss of traffic, so it was eventually demolished. Today the columns of the County Bridge and the TVA Bridge stand as relics of another era.

Most likely built by Thomas Jackson in 1810, McDonald's Mill was one of the area's earliest businesses. The McDonalds were the last owners of the mill. At one time it was known as Austin's Mill, which became the name of the community located a short distance south of Rogersville on the Holston River. TVA acquired the property in 1942, and the mill was torn down in 1966–1967. On the bluff across the road from the mill location stands a large two-story home known as the McDonald house.

The Burem Bridge was built in 1915 and spanned the Holston River in the Burem community. The bridge was a favorite spot for romance in the 1920s and 1930s. The Burem Bridge was a long one-lane bridge that was not adequate for the traffic by the 1960s. A modern two-lane bridge was built to replace the Burem Bridge and was named for local lawyer and congressman Bill Jenkins. Travelers now get to Burem, Kepler, and Beech Creek by crossing the William L. Jenkins Bridge.

Construction on the John Sevier Steam Plant started in 1952 and was finished in 1957. It stands on the Holston River at the site of the old Holston Tile Company/Weaver Brick Company plant. The plant has four coal-fired generating units and consumes 5,700 tons of coal per day. Now referred to as the John Sevier Fossil Plant, it can generate 5 billion kilowatt-hours of electricity per year, which is enough electricity to supply 350,000 homes.

Country stores were important to many of Rogersville's outlying communities until the late 1900s. Travel to Rogersville was not always practical, and the country store often served not only as a store, but also as a post office, a community center, and often as a place to loaf and catch up on the news. The Burem Store was located at the intersection of Burem and Tunnel Hill Roads. By the 1960s, ice cream and soft drinks were big sellers, as the signs indicate. Sadly, the Burem Store is now gone. (Then photograph from the Randy Ball collection.)

The Southern Railroad trestle spanned the Holston River about 2 miles south of Rogersville at Austin Mill. The bridge brought trains into Rogersville from the railroad center of Bulls Gap. The bridge was condemned in the 1970s but stood like a monument honoring past times for the next several decades. It was finally razed around 2000, leaving only a few of the columns standing near the banks of the Holston River. (Then photograph from the Randy Ball collection.)

CHAPTER 4

People and Events

As rich as Rogersville is in historical buildings, it is even more so in its people, who are the real treasures. They love celebrations and festivals, and will share their talents at any given opportunity. Making moonshine was once a popular activity for some of Hawkins County's citizens. In the 1950s, sheriff Howard Reeves, along with deputies Ed E. Price and Gordel White, found this moonshine still near Rogersville. (Denver Price.)

Fourth of July celebrations have always been popular in Rogersville. In the historical photograph, large flags flew from many buildings on Main Street, and the parade traveled from east to west, featuring many horse-drawn wagons. A welcome banner spanned the street near the town square. Large celebrations and parades have been held on most years. In 2008, horses and mules still had a place in the parade, but the route ran from west to east.

The people of Rogersville love their automobiles. The historical photograph depicts a young lady behind the wheel at the gas pumps of Rogan Motor Company, which also featured Mobil Oil among its products. In the 2008 image, an immaculately restored street rod is displayed in front of the Masonic Temple on Main Street during one of several summer "cruise-ins." Instituted in 2008, these festive events also featured live music on the town square.

First Row: Margaret Lipe, Faye Turnmyer, Sue Lawson, Barbara Davis, Sheila Weems. Second Row: Manager Imogene Jones, Katherine Lane, Bernice Poe, Sandra Brewer, Betty Davis, Coach Harold Pope.

Girls' basketball has been a favorite sport in Hawkins County. In the 1953 yearbook photograph above, the Rogersville High School Lady Warriors are ready for a great season. At that time, Rogersville High School was to be found in the current Rogersville Middle School location. The coach was Harold Pope. The 2008–2009 Cherokee High School Lady Chiefs are shown below. Mitzi Price is the head coach for the Lady Chiefs.

High school football is probably Rogersville's most popular sports. The games take on a festival atmosphere. For local fans, football games are something of a social event as well. The 1956 Rogersville High School (RHS) Warriors, shown below in this RHS yearbook photograph, were undefeated. In 1978, the school moved just outside of town, and the team became the Cherokee High School Chiefs and are shown above in action in the 2008 season opener against the new Grainer County High School.

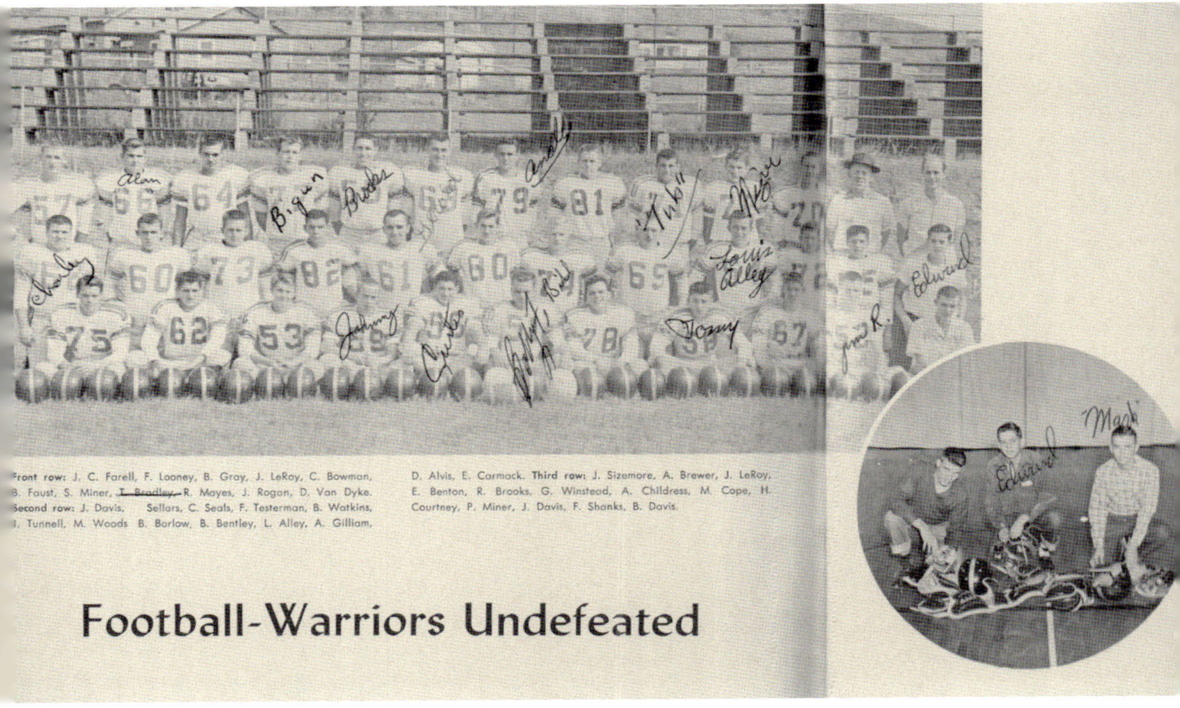

Music is an important part of life in Rogersville. The photograph below, labeled 1857, shows the Rogersville community band. Community or town bands were once common and would play occasional concerts and in parades. Today many students are introduced to music in the band programs of the public schools. In addition to general musical instruction, students perform in a concert band and a marching band. Above, some members of the Cherokee High School Marching Chiefs perform at the halftime of a 2008 football game.

The *Davy Crockett Outdoor Drama* was organized in 1966 after the success of the Hancock County drama *Walk into the Sunset*. The *Davy Crockett Outdoor Drama* was the brainchild of Marion Slaughter, Louise Rogers, and Mary Clay Lewis. The outdoor theater was built on Hasson Street. The show was realistic with horse-mounted soldiers and live cannon fire. The show closed in 1971 after four successful seasons. Today the Shakespeare and Friends Renaissance Faire continues the tradition of pageantry in Rogersville.

Rogersville is proud of its beautiful young ladies. In the 1960s, the Miss Holston Electric pageant was an annual event. The historical photograph shows the girls in the swimsuit portion of the pageant. There has not been a Miss Holston Electric pageant for several years, but Cherokee High School elects a homecoming queen every fall. Shown below at the 2008 homecoming game are the contestants in their formal gowns with their escorts, waiting to be introduced to an enthusiastic crowd. (Then photograph from Cary Lewis Barton.)

Over time, motor vehicles have become a mainstay in Rogersville parades, gradually replacing many of the horse-drawn wagons and buggies. Below, this highly decorated truck lead a section of a parade made up mostly of children through downtown Rogersville in the 1950s. In 2007, this vintage fire truck delighted the crows at the Fourth of July parade. This is near the town square intersection, and the Kyle house is seen in the background.

Below, these young musicians took a long enough break from picking to be photographed in the late 1800s. These youngsters were playing fiddle and guitar in the photograph, taken on a front porch in the Rogersville area. Keeping the tradition alive, Ashley Hilton plays mandolin on the town square at Heritage Days 2008. Her father, Duel, accompanied her on guitar, making this a special family moment.

Heritage Days is Rogersville's annual fall festival. The event draws thousands of visitors. The event features juried craftspeople, live music, and a variety of foods. The late "Doc Randall" Hoard of the Persia community performed his "Old Medicine Show" at one of the early Heritage Days Festivals. His act was well known, and he performed all over the country for many years. In 2008, a group of South American musicians had a booth and played an assortment of native instruments. (Then photograph from the Randy Ball collection.)

Rogersville once depended on agriculture as a leading industry, and its past history as a farming community has always been celebrated at Heritage Days. In 1981, this team of three mules drew the attention of festivalgoers. The Citizens Supply building is in the background. At Heritage Days 2008, the antique tractor exhibit was popular. Many area enthusiasts enjoy restoring old tractors, and the distinctive sound of a John Deere engine can be heard in Rogersville during the October event. (Then photograph from the Randy Ball collection.)

In the 1920s photograph below, automobiles were new to the streets of Rogersville. These two young men were out for a ride in a convertible when captured by the camera. Over the years, many local citizens have begun restoring antique cars. In the 2008 photograph at left, a beautifully restored auto is parked on Main Street during one of the monthly "cruise-ins." These events drew large crowds to the downtown area for festive Friday nights.

Musicians gathered at Ralph's Plumbing and Heating on Armstrong Road for a little picking and singing in the 1980s. Pictured at right are Albert "Pop" Davenport (mandolin), Paul Elkins (guitar), and Larry Bass (banjo). A weekly show, "Music Junction," was later organized and held at the parks and recreation building just off Main Street. "Music Junction" is held every Thursday night, and all area country, bluegrass, and gospel musicians are welcome. There is no admission charge. In the 2008 photograph, Ernie Graves is performing with the house band. (Then photograph from the Randy Ball collection.)

Cheerleaders have always been an important part of high school sports in Rogersville. At one time, there were not many opportunities for female athletes, and cheerleading was, and continues to be, an opportunity for young ladies to participate and express themselves. In the 1953 yearbook photograph of the Rogersville High School cheerleaders, it is obvious that styles have changed. In 2008, Amanda Williams of the Cherokee High School cheerleading squad shows that school spirit is still alive.

While many youngsters begin singing in church, high school has often provided additional opportunities. In the 1964 yearbook photograph, the Rogersville High School Glee Club is shown. Jerry Cole was the Glee Club sponsor. The 2004 Cherokee High School Choir is shown performing its annual concert. The choir's concerts and plays, under the direction of Justin Nelson, have become highly anticipated community events.

Baton twirlers were an important part of halftime shows at football games at Rogersville High School. This group of twirlers from the 1960s is posed in front of the high school; at present, Cherokee High School does not have a baton program. Today students at Cherokee High School have the opportunity to enroll in the ROTC. Members of the ROTC program have a strong presence at football games when they present the nation's flag during the pregame ceremonies. This ceremony was at the 2008 season opener against Grainger County High. (Historical photograph courtesy of Cary Lewis Barton.)

High school bands have long been a tradition in Rogersville, and the programs stayed strong when the new high school was built. Below, this 1970s Rogersville High School Marching Warriors Band is performing at the Rogersville High School field, which had stands on both sides. In the image taken in 2002, the Cherokee Marching Chiefs are shown performing at a late-season Cherokee High School game. The Cherokee High School stadium is known as "Big Red Valley."

The Fourth of July parade has always been a cause for celebration in Rogersville. American flags have always been displayed by patriotic citizens. In the 1907 photograph at left, two young ladies in a horse-drawn buggy are shown as the parade passed through the center of Rogersville. One lady identified is Fannie Bachman Summers. In 2006, on West Main Street near IPC Dennison, a group of Shriners delighted the crowd with their skills driving go-carts. Flags can be seen waving from the upper stories of the buildings in the historical image and from masts on the carts in the modern photograph.

The *Davy Crockett Outdoor Drama* enjoyed wide popularity during its run. The cast went on the road and is shown here at the Holiday Inn in Greeneville, Tennessee. Today the drama club at Cherokee High School enjoys a similar measure of fame. The club's plays draw large crowds and are performed over several days during the spring semester. Elaborate sets, beautiful music and singing, and long hours of practice have made the plays highly anticipated events. In 2005, *The Secret Garden* was performed. (Then photograph from Cary Lewis-Barton.)

Heritage Days has grown to become a regionally known event. Craft demonstrations have always played a big part in the event. Many Appalachian crafts have been shown to thousands of visitors over the decades. The late basket maker Lonnie Tallioferro was a fixture at early Heritage Days festivals. He is pictured at left in 1982 at his booth in front of the Hale Springs Inn. In 2007, Brenda Snell demonstrated her spinning skills in front of the local artist gallery. (Then photograph from the Randy Ball collection.)

Costumes add to special events in Rogersville. In the 1960s, frontier costumes graced the musicians in the *Davy Crockett Outdoor Drama*. In 2007, jester costumes were among the many seen at the Shakespeare and Friends Renaissance Faire. The annual event is held at the Crockett Springs Park. The fair features Celtic music, fire breathing, belly dancing, puppetry, and comedy. In early June each year, knights and damsels descend on Rogersville. (Then photograph from Cary Lewis-Barton.)

Many men from Rogersville have served their country with honor. A World War II memorial is located at the flagpole on the courthouse lawn. Among those named on the memorial is James Basil Smith, shown with his car while on leave near Rogersville. He lost his life in Austria just before the war ended. At Heritage Days 2008, a group of reenactors, including this young "soldier," paid tribute to World War II veterans with a display on the Masonic Temple lawn. (Then photograph from the Randy Ball collection.)

These two parades were photographed decades apart but from the same vantage point high above Main Street. In the historical photograph, the parade traveled from east to west, and the photograph was made looking west as the parade passed. The Hale Springs Inn is seen on the left. In 2002, the parade again traveled from east to west, but the parade was photographed looking east as the parade approached. Here the Cherokee High School Marching Band passes in front of the Mountain Star Mall.

These two images look to the past, present, and future. In the 1960s, the Miss Holston Electric Pageant was an annual event with young Rogersville beauty contestants vying for the honor. Though Holston Electric no longer holds this pageant, there are several other beauty contests, and the winners often participate in local parades. In 2008, this young lady was honored in the Fourth of July parade. Rogersville's past has been amazing, and the future looks bright. (Then photograph from Cary Lewis Barton.)

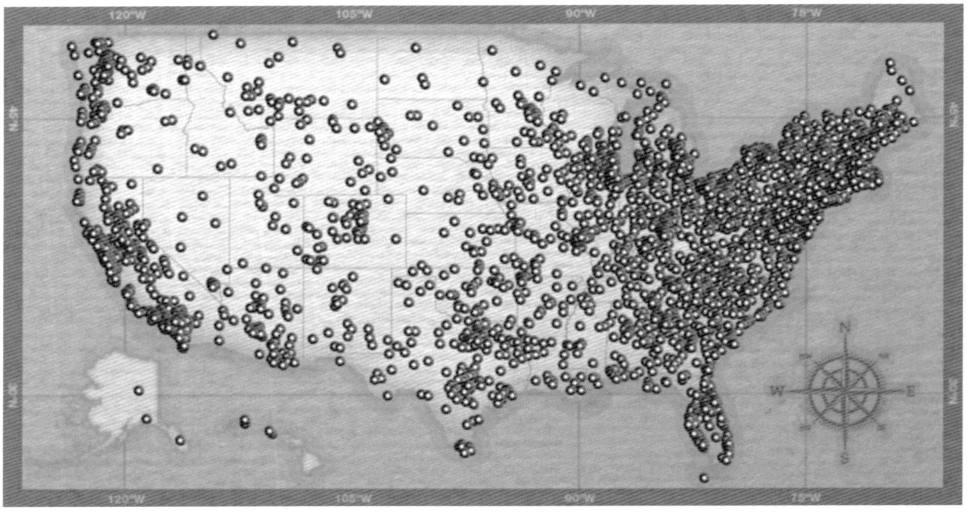